INFINITE BEING

The Effortless Journey to Self-Realization

ROBERT RUGG

Copyright © 2025 Robert Rugg

All rights reserved

No part of this publication may be reproduced, stored in a retrieval system, or transmitted, in any form or by any means—electronic, mechanical, photocopying, recording, or otherwise—without the prior written permission of the publisher, except in the case of brief quotations embodied in critical reviews and certain other noncommercial uses permitted by copyright law.

For permission requests, contact Effortless Being Publications, infinitebeingness1@gmail.com

ISBN: 979-8-3102-6007-8
Published by Effortless Being Publications

Disclaimer: The experiences and insights shared in this book are the author's own and intended to provide information and inspiration for personal growth and self-realization. It is not a substitute for professional advice, and the author does not assume any responsibility for any results or consequences related to the application of the information in this book.

*To my wife, for being my anchor of love, joy,
and unwavering support.*

*To my daughters, Brianna, Madison, and Abby, for
inspiring me with your boundless curiosity,
laughter, and light.*

*To David Bingham, for your profound words that revealed
the truth of infinite being and changed my life forever.*

*And to everyone seeking joy and clarity,
this book is for you.
May you always trust the magic of the universe
and know the beauty of living in the flow.*

CONTENTS

Foreword 7

Chapter 1: Introduction: Awakening to Your Infinite Nature 9

Chapter 2: From Seeking to Knowing: The Shift from Duality to Effortless Being............................14

Chapter 3: Why Effortless Being? Finding the Joy Beyond Struggle..20

Chapter 4: Intellectual vs. Experiential Knowing............24

Chapter 5: The Koshas Reimagined: Filters of Your Experience 30

Chapter 6: Disarming Doubt: Restoring Clarity in the Infinite Now...37

Chapter 7: Manifesting from Your Infinite Self................45

Chapter 8: Embracing the Eternal Now: Living in Direct, Unmediated Experience...................................52

Chapter 9: Integration: From Effortless Being to Engaged Living 59

Chapter 10: True Peace at Last: Living the Infinite Being Experience 66

Continue Your Journey with Additional Resources & a Personal Invitation 72

Acknowledgments 74

About the Author 76

Foreword

ONE OF THE MOST profound realizations on the path of awakening is that there is no path at all—only the effortless unfolding of what has always been. The search for truth, meaning, and fulfillment has long consumed spiritual seekers, yet the great paradox is that what we seek is already present. It has never been lost, only overlooked.

This book, *Infinite Being The Effortless Journey To Self-Realization*, is a powerful reminder of that truth. It is an invitation to let go of striving, to surrender the illusion of effort, and to simply rest in the awareness that is already here. Robert Rugg brings a clarity and ease to this exploration, guiding readers beyond the limitations of conditioned thinking and into the direct experience of their true nature.

ROBERT RUGG

Robert's approach is both profound and refreshingly lighthearted. He effortlessly weaves together deep spiritual wisdom with practical insights, making the realization of our infinite nature not only accessible but joyful. His words serve as a gentle nudge toward recognizing that life is not something to struggle with or control, but something to allow—something to flow with in complete trust. The essence of this book aligns deeply with the understanding I have shared in my own journey.

The recognition of our ever-present, impersonal being—the infinite awareness that we are—transforms every aspect of life. When the struggle falls away, what remains is peace, joy, and an effortless unfolding of experience.

With love,

David Bingham

Chapter 1: Introduction
Awakening to Your Infinite Nature

Why This Book?

I REMEMBER DRIVING down long, empty roads and noticing the tired, drawn faces of fellow travelers. In those quiet moments, a single thought emerged: "There has to be more to life than this." I could see it in the eyes of those around me—a deep yearning for something beyond the mundane cycle of work, worry, and weariness.

It was then that I sensed an inner stirring: life was meant to be fun, joyful, and effortless. This book is born from that very recognition—a call to awaken to the truth that beneath every thought, every fleeting emotion, and every stressful moment lies an infinite, unchanging presence.

This book isn't about chasing after happiness or manifesting material abundance through hard work and striving. Instead, it is an invitation to remember what you truly are: an infinite being whose natural state is effortless, expansive joy. The pages that follow are my humble attempt to share the insights I've gleaned along my own journey—a journey from seeking to knowing, from the endless questions of the mind to the serene, all-encompassing awareness of what you are.

The Promise of Effortless Being

Imagine a life where you no longer need to force or chase; where each moment unfolds with a natural, unburdened grace. In my early years, I believed that success meant constant striving—crafting elaborate vision boards, setting lofty goals, and never being satisfied until I reached that next milestone. But along the way, I discovered something far more profound: **Effortless Being.**

Effortless Being is the state of pure awareness that underlies all experiences. It is the deep, unshakeable knowing that you are not limited by the passing thoughts of the mind, nor are you defined by the temporary roles you play in the world. When you align with your infinite nature, the world no longer feels like a battleground of stress and struggle. Instead, life becomes a fluid, playful adventure where every experience—whether joyous or challenging—is welcomed as a natural unfolding of the eternal now.

In these pages, you will learn how to quiet the mind's incessant chatter and step into the spacious, peaceful presence that is your birthright. You'll discover that true power comes not from exerting effort but from surrendering to the natural flow of existence—a flow that effortlessly brings forth the gifts of creativity, love, and abundance.

Overview of the Journey Ahead

This book is structured as a map for your journey from the restless search for meaning to the serene recognition of what you truly are. Here's a glimpse of what lies ahead:

- ❖ **From Seeking to Knowing:** We begin by exploring the shift from a life defined by endless seeking to a state of knowing your infinite nature. Through personal anecdotes and practical insights, you'll see how the illusion of separation dissolves when you remember that you are the infinite being having a human experience.

- ❖ **Finding Joy Beyond Struggle:** Next, we dive into why effortless being matters. Remember that inner question on the road? We'll examine how that burning need for something more can lead you to a profound realization—that life, at its core, is meant to be joyful and free from unnecessary struggle.

- ❖ **Exploring the Layers of Your Experience:** The journey continues as we reimagine the ancient concept of the Koshas—the filters through which you perceive reality. We'll look at how a top-down perspective can empower you to choose the lens through which you experience life, releasing you from the confines of dualistic thinking.

- ❖ **Restoring Clarity in the Infinite Now:** Doubt, stress, and negative emotions can all act as invitations pulling you back into a state of separation. We'll learn practical tools to decline these invitations, gently returning your focus to your ever-present, unchanging awareness.

- ❖ **Effortless Manifestation:** As you begin to reside more fully in the state of infinite being, the process of manifesting your desires becomes less about effort and more about aligning with the natural flow of life. Discover how to tune into the right "channel" of thought—one that brings forth your highest joy and potential.

- ❖ **Living in Direct, Unmediated Experience:** Finally, we'll explore the concept of the Eternal Now, where the past and future are seen as mere thoughts, and every moment is an opportunity for direct, unmediated experience—a never-ending movie in which you are both the observer and the creator.

Throughout this book, I invite you to join me in rediscovering the inherent ease and joy of simply being. The journey is not about acquiring something new, but about recognizing the eternal truth that you already are—the infinite being whose nature is blissful, creative, and utterly free.

Welcome to your awakening. Let's begin the journey together.

Chapter 2

From Seeking to Knowing:

The Shift from Duality to Effortless Being

The Restless Search for More
FOR SO LONG, I WAS caught in a relentless quest—seeking answers, chasing after an elusive happiness that always seemed just out of reach. That endless seeking was the very hallmark of the dualistic world: a world defined by separation, struggle, and the illusion of a limited self.

The Illusion of the Separate Self
In our daily lives, we are bombarded with messages that tell us we are separate entities—individuals with distinct stories, likes, and dislikes. This separation creates an internal narrative that convinces us we must work hard, strive relentlessly, and chase after fleeting pleasures. In

that narrative, every moment of dissatisfaction fuels the search for something better.

But here's the truth: that "separate self" is nothing more than a thought, a transient story that the mind constructs. The very act of seeking, of feeling incomplete, is born from a mistaken identification with this limited self-image.

The Moment of Recognition

Then came a turning point—a moment when the inner voice became unmistakably clear. I realized that the feeling of "more" wasn't something to be obtained through effort or external pursuits. It was already present in the vast, open space of my awareness.

In that instant, the phrase "I am the infinite being having a human experience" didn't just sound like a catchy spiritual quote; it was a direct pointer to what I truly was. I began to see that every experience, every thought and emotion, was simply unfolding in the infinite now. There was no need to strive or struggle; everything was as it should be.

Embracing Effortless Being

This realization sparked a profound shift. I moved from a state of perpetual seeking into one of deep knowing. Instead of trying to force myself into a role defined by limitations, I learned to simply rest in the awareness of what I am. It became clear that the joy I had been chasing was not hidden in some far-off goal—it was already present, waiting to be recognized in the here and now.

Effortless Being means trusting that every moment unfolds with a natural, unburdened grace. It means recognizing that the mind's endless chatter is not who you are but rather a set of transient thoughts drifting through the vast space of your being. In this state, life transforms into a playful adventure where the unexpected becomes a source of delight instead of dread.

When you let go of the idea of a separate, striving self, you begin to experience life directly—with a lightness that makes every moment feel spontaneous and free.

Practical Steps to Shift from Seeking to Knowing

While the transformation is ultimately an inner recognition, here are a few practical insights to support your shift:

- ➤ **Pause and Observe:** When you find yourself caught in the cycle of seeking, pause. Take a few deep breaths and observe your thoughts without judgment. Notice that you are not your thoughts; you are the awareness in which they appear.
- ➤ **Affirm Your Infinite Nature:** Remind yourself, "I am the infinite being having a human experience." Allow this phrase to dissolve the boundaries of your personal story, letting the truth of your expansive nature come to the forefront.
- ➤ **Release the Need for More:** Recognize that the endless chase for something "better" is an invitation from the dualistic mind. Gently decline this invitation by focusing on the simplicity of being—where everything is already complete.
- ➤ **Reflect on Moments of Joy:** Look back on times when you felt truly alive, free, and joyful. Realize that these moments are not rare exceptions but glimpses of your true nature. Use them as anchors to return to your innate state of Effortless Being.

The Transformation in Daily Life

Once you begin to know what you are rather than endlessly chasing who you think you should be, everyday life takes on a new texture. The pressures of work, relationships, and societal expectations begin to lose their grip. Instead of viewing challenges as obstacles to overcome, you see them as natural parts of a flowing experience. The inner tension melts away, replaced by a sense of playfulness and wonder.

You start noticing that the joy you once thought was unattainable isn't hidden in external achievements or material success—it's woven into every moment of existence. Whether you are driving on a lonely highway or sharing laughter with friends, the experience of Effortless Being infuses even the most ordinary moments with profound meaning.

Knowing What You Are

The journey from seeking to knowing is both subtle and transformative. It is not about acquiring something new, but about uncovering the vast, infinite presence that has always been within you. When you stop identifying with the limited self and instead rest in the recognition of your true nature, you step into a life that is vibrant, joyful, and utterly effortless.

This chapter invites you to take a moment, to look beyond the transient stories of the mind, and to recognize the timeless, expansive being that you truly are. In doing so, you open the door to a life where every experience, whether joyous or challenging, is part of the magnificent unfolding of the infinite now.

Chapter 3

Why Effortless Being?

Finding the Joy Beyond Struggle

Introduction: A Question Born at Work
I STILL REMEMBBER watching people at work—observing the tired faces, the heavy postures, and the silent resignation that seemed to fill the room. Every weary expression appeared to ask, "Is this life really all there is?"

It was as if each individual, caught in the grind of endless tasks, was silently pleading for something deeper—a life not defined by ceaseless struggle but by genuine joy and possibility.

That question, born at work, became the spark that ignited my journey toward discovering what effortless being truly means.

The Inner Feeling that Life is Supposed to Be Fun

Deep inside, beneath the weight of daily routines and responsibilities, there was a gentle yet persistent inner voice reminding me that life was meant to be fun. I began to notice that beyond the hustle of work, the stress of expectations, and the mundane routines, there lay an unexplored reservoir of joy—a state of being where laughter, playfulness, and spontaneity were not rare commodities but natural expressions of our true nature.

In those moments of quiet reflection, I experienced flashes of an inner lightness—a recognition that the rigid structures of our dualistic world were not the only way to live. This realization slowly transformed my perspective: I started to see that the constant battle with life's challenges was not a requirement, but rather an invitation to shift into an infinite, effortless state.

The journey became less about accumulating achievements and more about rediscovering that childlike wonder and delight that is our birthright.

Aligning with the Infinite, Effortless State

The more I questioned the endless struggle, the more I realized that my true nature isn't about hard work or forceful striving—it's about aligning with the infinite being that I already am. In that shift, I learned to see myself not as a separate, limited individual, but as an expression of timeless, boundless consciousness.

This alignment is not about denying the human experience; it's about experiencing life from a place where joy, spontaneity, and creativity flow effortlessly. By stepping away from the constant need to "do" and instead resting in the awareness of what I truly am, I found that challenges and stressors lose their grip. They become nothing more than passing thoughts and sensations—each an invitation to return to the inherent peace that underlies all of existence.

When we allow ourselves to dwell in this effortless state, we also tap into an infinite source of creativity and possibility. Life's obstacles become opportunities to experiment, to laugh at the absurdity of our past limitations, and to create new experiences with a light heart. It's a dynamic, playful dance between our inner truth and the outer world—a process that invites us to live each moment as a celebration of what we are.

Conclusion: Embracing the Call for Effortless Living

Chapter 3 is an invitation to reframe the way we experience life. The tired faces on the road were not just signs of exhaustion; they were a call to awaken—to remember that deep inside, life is supposed to be fun. When you begin to align with your infinite, effortless nature, you no longer see the world as a series of struggles, but as a canvas of endless possibility.

This chapter challenges you to step away from the conventional measures of success and to ask instead, "What is life really about?" In answering that question, you will uncover that your true state is not burdened by effort or strain but is naturally joyful, creative, and expansive. It is a reminder that the journey toward effortless being begins with a single, transformative question—and that question is: "Is this all there is?"

Embrace the call. Allow your inner light to guide you back to the effortless state that has always been yours. The adventure of discovering your true, infinite self is not about accumulating more; it's about shedding the layers of struggle to reveal the simple, unadorned joy of being.

ROBERT RUGG

Chapter 4

Intellectual vs. Experiential Knowing

WHEN WE FIRST EMBARK on the journey toward effortless being, much of what we gather about our true nature comes from books, teachings, and discussions. These provide us with intellectual maps of reality. But the real transformation occurs when we move beyond concepts to direct, embodied experience.

In this chapter, we explore the shift from knowing something in the head to living it in the heart and body.

Moving Beyond the Mind's Illusions

Our mind is a brilliant tool. It generates ideas, constructs theories, and even points us toward the possibility of awakening. Yet, the mind also creates illusions. It wraps us in layers of thoughts, beliefs, and expectations that can obscure the simple truth of who we truly are.

Consider how the mind can endlessly debate ideas like "Who am I?" or "What is reality?" Even when these questions are answered intellectually, a subtle restlessness often remains. This is because intellectual knowing remains at the level of concepts: it is always one step removed from direct experience.

When we try to define our true nature solely through words and theories, we risk getting trapped in the very dualities we seek to transcend. The mind's language is inherently dualistic—it divides, labels, and categorizes. In doing so, it can make us feel separated from the infinite, undivided awareness that is our true essence.

Moving beyond these mental illusions means recognizing that while the mind can point to a truth, it is not the vehicle through which the truth is ultimately experienced. True knowing comes when we stop "thinking about" our awareness and instead allow our being to simply be. It is here that the rich, effortless state of being—untouched by the conceptual chatter—reveals itself.

Embracing Direct, Embodied Experience

Imagine standing at the edge of a calm lake at sunrise. You might read about the beauty of the scene, or listen to someone describe the gentle light and soft ripples. Yet, the true wonder is only felt when you step into that moment with your entire being—when you feel the cool air, hear the silence, and witness the radiance with your own eyes.

This is the difference between intellectual knowing and experiential knowing. Direct experience is immediate. It is the embodied, visceral recognition of what it means to be effortlessly alive.

Embracing direct experience involves tuning into the sensations of your body, the subtle shifts in your emotional state, and the quiet whisper of your inner awareness. It means learning to listen to the body's wisdom instead of getting caught up in mental narratives.

When you allow yourself to fully experience a moment—whether it's the joy of a shared laugh or the quiet contemplation during a solitary walk—you begin to see that your true nature isn't an idea or a concept. It is the constant, silent presence behind every experience.

Practical exercises—like mindfulness meditation, mindful breathing, or simply pausing to observe your surroundings without judgment—can help shift your focus from the mind's relentless analysis to the felt experience of being. This is where transformation happens: in the rich interplay between sensation, emotion, and pure awareness.

The Role of Self-Inquiry in Uncovering Your True Nature

Self-inquiry is the tool that bridges the gap between intellectual understanding and direct experience. It is not about accumulating more knowledge or debating abstract theories. Rather, self-inquiry is a gentle, persistent asking of the question, "What is it that I am?"

When you ask this question deeply and repeatedly—with sincerity and without expectation—the mind begins to quiet, and what remains is the pure, unadorned awareness that has always been there. This process is similar to watching a movie unfold on the screen of your consciousness: you observe the narrative without getting entangled in it.

By questioning each thought and emotion as it arises—wondering if it truly defines you—you gradually learn to identify the subtle difference between the passing content of your mind and the ever-present witness of awareness. With time and practice, this self-inquiry transforms from a mental exercise into an experiential shift. You begin to feel your true nature not as an abstract concept, but as the living, breathing, effortless presence that is your natural state.

Tools for self-inquiry might include journaling, guided meditations focused on the question "What am I?" or even simple reflection during daily activities. The goal is to dissolve the false sense of a separate "me" that clings to thoughts, emotions, and physical sensations. Instead, you allow yourself to rest as the infinite, unchanging awareness that simply observes life as it unfolds.

Conclusion

In Chapter 4, we've begun to unravel the limitations of intellectual knowledge and highlighted the beauty of direct, embodied experience. When we move beyond the mind's illusions, we find that true knowing is not something we acquire—it is something we remember.

Self-inquiry becomes the gateway to this remembering, enabling you to peel away the layers of mental chatter and rediscover the effortless, infinite nature that you truly are. As you practice embracing direct experience, you will notice that life no longer appears as a series of challenges to overcome but as a continuous, effortless unfolding of moments in which your true self shines through.

INFINITE BEING

Take a moment now. Pause, breathe, and simply notice.

In that quiet space, where the mind's distractions fade away, you are left with one undeniable truth: you are the infinite, effortless being. And this realization is the beginning of living from the deepest well of joy and clarity.

Chapter 5

The Koshas Reimagined:

Filters of Your Experience

IN OUR JOURNEY TOWARD effortless being, we encounter the Koshas—traditionally understood as the five layers of human existence. These layers have long served as guides for understanding the nature of our experience, from the physical to the sublime.

In this chapter, we will first revisit the traditional (bottom-up) model of the Koshas, then explore a new (top-down) perspective that empowers you to choose your lens, and finally introduce practical exercises designed to help shift your focus toward a more expansive, effortless awareness.

The Traditional (Bottom-Up) Model of the Koshas

Historically, the Koshas have been presented as a sequential ascent through layers that include:

1. Annamaya Kosha (The Physical Body): This is the outermost layer—the body that consumes food, moves, and interacts with the world. It represents the tangible, material aspect of our existence.
2. Pranamaya Kosha (The Energy or Vital Body): This layer encompasses the flow of energy, represented by breath and life force. It underlies our physical sensations and emotions.
3. Manomaya Kosha (The Mental Body): Here reside our thoughts, perceptions, and emotions—the dynamic yet ever-changing mental activities that color our experience.
4. Vijnanamaya Kosha (The Body of Wisdom): This deeper layer is associated with intuition, insight, and wisdom. It is the part of our experience where knowledge is not merely learned but deeply known.
5. Anandamaya Kosha (The Bliss Body): The innermost layer is pure, unmediated bliss. It is a state of effortless being—a constant, unchanging

background of joy and contentment that exists beyond the fluctuations of thoughts and emotions.

In the traditional model, one is encouraged to work through these layers in a "bottom-up" fashion. The idea is that by gradually transcending the limitations of the physical and mental, one can eventually access the bliss of the innermost self. Although this approach has guided spiritual seekers for millennia, it can also feel daunting—suggesting that self-realization is something to be earned through continuous effort.

A New (Top-Down) Perspective: Choosing Your Lens

Imagine instead that you are already the embodiment of bliss and infinite awareness. In this new perspective, the Koshas are not stages to be achieved but filters through which your infinite being expresses itself.

Rather than laboriously climbing upward from the physical to the blissful core, you have the innate freedom to choose which layer or lens you wish to experience at any given moment.

- ❖ Recognize Your Default State: At your core, you are not the limited, struggling individual—you are the timeless, effortless being. This is the state of

Anandamaya Kosha, the bliss body that is always present, regardless of external circumstances.

- ❖ View the Layers as Tools, Not Barriers: The lower Koshas (physical, energy, and mental) are simply tools or filters that shape how you experience life. They do not define you; they merely color your experience. When you recognize these layers as temporary and relative, you can begin to see that your true nature is not constrained by them.

- ❖ Choose Your Perspective Intentionally: With this top-down approach, you are empowered to "tune" your experience. Whether you need the grounding presence of the physical body, the vibrancy of the energy field, or the clarity of the mind, you can choose the lens that best serves you in the moment. This is the essence of effortless being—living from a place of abundance rather than scarcity, playfulness rather than struggle.

This perspective invites you to shift your attention away from trying to "fix" or overcome the limitations of the lower layers. Instead, you simply acknowledge them as part of the rich tapestry of your experience while always returning to the awareness that is your true self.

Practical Exercises for Shifting Your Focus

To help you integrate this new perspective, consider these practical exercises:

1. **Mindful Tuning**
   - Sit quietly and take a few deep, conscious breaths.
   - Notice any sensations, thoughts, or emotions that arise. Rather than identifying with them, simply observe them as passing phenomena.
   - Ask yourself, "Which Kosha am I experiencing right now?" Notice if your experience is dominated by physical tension, energetic fluctuations, or mental chatter.
   - Gently remind yourself: "I am the infinite being behind all these layers." Allow this thought to recenter you.

2. **Language Shift Exercise**
   - When you notice yourself saying, "I am tired" or "I am overwhelmed," pause and reframe the thought.
   - Instead, say, "There is awareness of tiredness" or "There is impersonal energy of overwhelm arising."

- This subtle linguistic shift helps break the identification with the lower layers and reconnects you to the state of effortless being.

3. **Visualization Practice**
    - Close your eyes and visualize your Koshas as layers of light. See the outer layers as softer, more malleable colors that can be shifted at will.
    - Visualize a bright, steady light at your core—the light of your true, infinite nature.
    - Imagine this light radiating outward, gently transforming the outer layers. Feel the shift as you consciously choose to "see through" the filters to your inner bliss.

4. **Daily Check-In**
    - Throughout your day, take moments to pause and ask yourself, "How am I experiencing life right now? Am I aligned with my infinite being?"
    - Use these check-ins to notice any recurring patterns or latent tendencies that pull you into a limited perspective.

- Journal briefly about these moments to reinforce your ability to recognize and then let go of these invitations back into duality.

Chapter 6

Disarming Doubt:

Restoring Clarity in the Infinite Now

DOUBT IS A NATURAL part of the human experience—even after awakening to your infinite nature. In this chapter, we explore the nature of doubt as it arises after self-realization, examine how stress, negative emotions, and those persistent "invitations" can pull you back into the dualistic matrix, and offer practical tools for declining these invitations and restoring your presence in the Infinite Now.

The Nature of Doubt After Awakening

Even as we awaken to the truth of our infinite being, doubt does not vanish overnight. It lingers as a subtle echo of the old, conditioned mind. In our awakened state, doubt often manifests in two distinct forms:

- ➢ Residual Doubt: The questioning of our newfound state "Am I really free?" or "How can this be all there is?" These questions arise from years of identifying with a limited, separate self.
- ➢ Conditioned Doubt: A lingering voice from the past, steeped in fear and scarcity, that occasionally reminds us of our old limitations. This voice may say, "What if I slip back into my old ways?" or "Can I really maintain this clarity?"

Both forms of doubt serve as invitations from the dualistic matrix. They seek to re-establish the narrative of separation and struggle. Yet, when viewed from the perspective of your true nature—pure, effortless presence—these doubts are nothing more than transient thoughts that arise and pass away.

How Stress, Negative Emotions, and "Invitations" Arise

The dualistic matrix is an intricate web of energetic patterns designed to capture your attention. Stress, negative emotions, and intrusive "invitations" to fall back into old patterns are the matrix's way of keeping you identified with the limited, conditioned self.

They emerge through several channels:

- ❖ **Stress and Negative Emotions**: When you begin to tap into your infinite nature, the mind sometimes reacts with resistance. Old fears and insecurities surface, creating a sensation of contraction. This stress can come from external events—a challenging conversation or an unexpected setback—but more often it arises from within, as the conditioned mind struggles to let go of its familiar narratives.

- ❖ **Energetic Invitations:** These are the subtle triggers that the dualistic matrix uses to draw you back into the realm of separation. They might manifest as nagging thoughts, sudden bouts of anxiety, or emotional swings that seem to have no clear origin. Each invitation is essentially a reminder of the old self, a call to invest energy in fear, doubt, and limitation.

- ❖ **The Role of the Demiurge**: On an even deeper level, these invitations are orchestrated by what can be understood as the energetic matrix—the demiurge. This parasitic intelligence thrives on the energy generated by negative emotions and resistance. It presents challenges and obstacles that are designed to keep you engaged in the cycle of struggle and suffering.

Recognizing that these reactions are not a sign of failure, but rather a natural part of the process, is the first step in disarming doubt. You begin to see that every stressful thought or emotion is an invitation that you have the power to decline.

Tools for Declining the Invitations and Restoring Presence

To remain anchored in the Infinite Now, it is essential to have practical tools that help you decline these invitations and restore your clarity. Here are several strategies to support your journey:

1. Awareness and Observation

- Pause and Notice: When you sense doubt or negative emotion arising, pause. Take a deep breath and allow yourself to simply observe the sensation without judgment. Recognize that it is merely a thought or feeling passing through your field of awareness.

- o Label the Invitation: Gently label the experience as an "invitation" from the dualistic matrix. For example, you might say to yourself, "There is an invitation to doubt," or "I notice a feeling of stress inviting me back to separation."

2. Impersonal Language

- o Reframe Your Experience: Instead of saying "I am anxious" or "I am doubtful," shift to impersonal language. Say, "There is awareness of anxiety arising," or "There is a thought of doubt present." This subtle shift helps detach your identity from these fleeting states, reminding you that they do not define who you truly are.

- o Practice Regularly: Make a habit of checking in with yourself throughout the day. When you notice personalizing language, pause and reframe your inner dialogue. Over time, this practice strengthens your ability to remain rooted in effortless being.

3. Direct Presence Practices

- o Mindful Breathing: Use mindful breathing techniques to anchor your attention in the present moment. Focus solely on the sensation of your breath entering and leaving your body. With each exhale, imagine releasing the tension and doubts that are inviting you back into the old patterns.

- Body Scan Meditation: Periodically perform a body scan meditation to become aware of any physical sensations linked to stress or doubt. By scanning from head to toe, you can identify areas of contraction and consciously invite a sense of ease and spaciousness into those areas.
- Visualization: Visualize your true nature as a vast, unchanging field of light or infinite space. Imagine that every negative thought or emotion is a small cloud passing over an endless sky of awareness. This visualization reinforces the understanding that, like the sky, your true nature remains constant and unaffected by temporary phenomena.

4. Cultivating Gratitude and Joy

- Shift Your Focus: When negative invitations arise, counterbalance them by recalling moments of joy, gratitude, or inner peace. Reflect on the aspects of life that remind you of your infinite being—the beauty of nature, a kind gesture from a friend, or even the simple pleasure of a quiet moment.

- Gratitude Journaling: Maintain a gratitude journal where you record moments of effortless being and instances when you successfully declined an invitation. Over time, this practice creates a positive feedback loop that reinforces your alignment with the Infinite Now.

5. Self-Inquiry and Reflection

- Ask Empowering Questions: Regularly engage in self-inquiry. Ask yourself questions like, "What is the nature of this doubt? Where is it coming from?" or "Can I allow this thought to pass without subscribing to it?" Let these questions guide you back to the awareness of your true nature.

- Reflect on Direct Experience: Remind yourself that all experiences, even those of doubt and stress, are temporary and arise within the unchanging field of your being. Reflect on past experiences where you were able to recognize and let go of such invitations, reinforcing your trust in the process.

Conclusion

In the realm of effortless being, doubt is not an enemy but a signpost—an invitation to return to the Infinite Now. By understanding the nature of these invitations, recognizing the mechanisms of stress and negative emotions, and applying practical tools like mindful awareness, impersonal language, and gratitude practices, you can disarm doubt and restore clarity.

Each moment offers you the opportunity to decline the pull of the dualistic matrix and choose the peace, joy, and expansiveness that are your birthright. In doing so, you affirm your identity not as a limited individual, but as the timeless, infinite being that you truly are.

Remember: every invitation you decline is a victory for your true nature. As you continue on this journey, let the clarity of the Infinite Now be your constant guide, and know that you are always free to rest in the effortless, expansive awareness of who—rather, *what*—you are.

Chapter 7
Manifesting from Your Infinite Self

MANIFESTATION ISN'T about grinding day after day, forcing outcomes with sheer willpower or elaborate vision boards. It's about tuning into your inherent, infinite nature—the effortless state of being that has always been your foundation—and allowing your reality to emerge naturally from that source. In this chapter, we explore how to rethink the Law of Attraction, shift from striving to effortless creation, and master the energy game by choosing the best "channel" for your thoughts.

Rethinking the Law of Attraction

Traditional teachings on the Law of Attraction often emphasize visualizing a desired outcome, feeling as though you already have it, and then working relentlessly to bring it into your life. While these practices can spark excitement, they sometimes inadvertently lead to strain, frustration, and the sense that you must "earn" your desires. Here's how to reframe your understanding:

❖ Beyond the Effort:

Recognize that your infinite self already contains all that you need. Manifestation isn't about generating something new or filling a void; it's about revealing what is already present in your being.

❖ Alignment Over Accumulation:

Instead of accumulating desires and chasing after material or external outcomes, focus on aligning with your natural state of ease. When you are fully present in your infinite nature, the need to force a specific outcome diminishes.

❖ Trusting the Process:

Understand that the process of creation is as natural as breathing. Your role isn't to manipulate the universe but to tune into its frequency. When you embody the truth that you are already complete, manifestations emerge effortlessly as an expression of your inner state.

By rethinking the Law of Attraction from the perspective of infinite being, you move away from a mindset of striving and enter a realm where creation is as effortless as a ripple on a still pond.

Shifting from Striving to Effortless Creation

The habitual approach to manifestation often involves hard work, excessive planning, and a constant striving for more. Yet, this very effort reinforces the separation—the idea that you must do something to "be" or "have" something.

Effortless creation, on the other hand, is about surrender and flow. Here's how you can shift your approach:

❖ **Letting Go of the "Need":**

When you release the compulsive need to achieve a particular outcome, you create space for something far greater. Recognize that every moment you spend struggling is a moment lost in the flow of your infinite being.

❖ **The Art of Surrender:**

Surrender does not mean giving up—it means allowing life to unfold naturally. Trust that your infinite self, when expressed in the world, will manifest exactly what is in alignment with your highest truth.

- ❖ **Effortless Action:**

When you operate from a state of effortless being, actions arise spontaneously. They are guided not by the push of the ego but by the gentle pull of your inner intelligence. This shift from doing to being changes the quality of your creative expression.

- ❖ **Embracing the Process:**

Appreciate the journey of creation as much as the destination. When you view every experience as a playful unfolding of your true nature, even setbacks become opportunities for growth and deeper alignment.

This new approach transforms manifestation from a battle against the current into a graceful dance with the flow of life. By letting go of strenuous effort, you allow your natural, creative essence to shine forth.

The Energy Game: Choosing the Best "Channel" for Your Thoughts

Every thought you entertain has a vibrational quality, and the channel through which you direct your energy determines the experiences that manifest in your life. Think of it as an energy game where you are both the player and the observer.

Here are ways to choose your channels wisely:

- ❖ **Understanding Your Frequency:**

Your infinite self radiates a frequency of love, joy, and boundless possibility. When you invest your energy in thoughts that mirror this frequency, you naturally attract experiences that resonate with your true nature. Conversely, dwelling on fear, doubt, or scarcity channels lower-energy experiences.

- ❖ **The Invitation to Choose:**

Every thought is an invitation—to either join a "party" of high vibrational, expansive experiences or to descend into a lower state of contraction. Learn to recognize these invitations early. Ask yourself: "Is this thought in alignment with the infinite being I am, or is it a relic of old conditioning?"

- ❖ **Practical Techniques:**
  - Mindful Monitoring: Regularly check in with yourself. Notice the dominant tone of your thoughts—are they uplifting or limiting?
  - Reframing Techniques: When a negative thought arises, consciously reframe it using impersonal language. Instead of "I am

anxious," say "There is awareness of anxiety." This subtle shift can help defuse the emotional charge of the thought.

- o Affirmation and Visualization: Cultivate affirmations that resonate with your infinite self. Visualize your inner light expanding and enveloping your thoughts, gently transforming them into channels of higher energy.

❖ **Consistency is Key:**

The more you practice choosing your thought channels consciously, the more your entire energetic field shifts. Over time, you'll notice that effortless, high-vibrational thoughts become your default mode, while lower-energy states arise less frequently and lose their grip quickly.

By mastering the energy game, you take control of the creative process. Instead of being a passive receiver of whatever thoughts come your way, you become an active co-creator—selecting, refining, and directing your mental energy to manifest the reality that truly reflects your infinite nature.

Conclusion

Manifesting from your infinite self is not about adding more effort to your life but about aligning with the inherent perfection of your being.

When you rethink the Law of Attraction, shift from striving to effortless creation, and consciously choose the best channels for your thoughts, you unlock a new realm of possibility. In this state, manifestation becomes an expression of who you already are—limitless, joyful, and effortlessly creative.

As you integrate these insights into your daily practice, you'll find that life unfolds with a natural grace. Each moment becomes a co-creation with the universe, guided by the energy of your true self. Embrace this process, trust in your infinite nature, and watch as your reality transforms into a living reflection of effortless being.

Chapter 8

Embracing the Eternal Now:

Living in Direct, Unmediated Experience

IN THIS CHAPTER, WE dive deep into the nature of time, the power of immediate awareness, and how life unfolds as an ever-changing, yet ever-present movie. This exploration is not merely theoretical—it is an invitation to shift your inner lens, so that you can fully inhabit the profound and liberating state of "now."

How the Past and Future Exist in the Now
Our conventional understanding of time divides our experience into past, present, and future. Yet, when you begin to explore the realm of direct, unmediated experience, you start to see that these divisions are mental constructs—filters imposed by the mind. In truth,

everything you experience, whether it be a memory of yesterday or an anticipation of tomorrow, always manifests in the present moment.

The Illusion of Linear Time

The mind habitually categorizes experiences as either "before" or "after." However, when you rest in the state of pure awareness, you begin to notice that every thought, memory, or anticipation arises right here, right now.

The past is simply a collection of images and sensations that have been stored in memory, and the future is a projection of hopes, fears, and expectations. Both are accessed through the medium of the present.

Integration Through Presence

Consider a moment when you recall a cherished memory. Although it belongs to the past, its essence—its joy, its pain, its meaning—reemerges in your current awareness.

Similarly, when you imagine the future, you are not stepping into a new reality but rather recalling potentials that are already woven into the fabric of your being. Every "future" thought is, in fact, a present experience, waiting to be acknowledged with clarity.

Practical Insight

- ❖ Try this simple exercise: pause for a moment and close your eyes. Notice any thoughts that refer to something past or future.

- ❖ As you become aware of them, gently return your focus to the present. Recognize that the true essence of your experience is always here.

Over time, this practice dissolves the habit of living in the confines of a linear timeline, revealing the timelessness of your infinite nature.

The Power of Immediate Awareness

Immediate awareness is the doorway to the eternal now. It is a state of direct perception that is free from the layers of interpretation, judgment, and memory that the mind habitually applies to every moment.

Witnessing Without Interference

In immediate awareness, you become the observer of your experiences without the interference of thoughts or stories. This state is characterized by a gentle, yet unwavering clarity—where you simply notice what is, without adding any narrative.

In this pure state, there is no "me" and "other." There is only the expansive, impersonal awareness that is the backdrop of all experience.

The Unfiltered Reality

When you practice immediate awareness, you encounter reality as it is—vivid, dynamic, and full of possibility. The textures of life become more apparent: the play of light and shadow, the subtle shifts in sound, the rise and fall of emotions.

Each sensation and thought is experienced directly, without being clouded by the mind's tendency to categorize or evaluate.

Cultivating the Habit:

The power of immediate awareness lies in its ability to ground you in the present moment. Regular meditation, mindful breathing, or simply pausing throughout the day to check in with your inner state can transform the way you experience life. Over time, this practice not only enhances clarity and inner peace but also empowers you to navigate challenges with a calm, centered presence.

Life as an Ever-Unfolding Movie

Imagine for a moment that life is like a movie—a rich, intricate narrative that unfolds scene by scene. In this analogy, you are both the viewer and the creator, witnessing the drama, comedy, and mystery of existence without becoming entangled in the storyline.

The Director and the Audience:

In the movie of life, the script is constantly being written and rewritten by the interplay of your thoughts, emotions, and actions. Yet, there is a crucial distinction: while the characters (the thoughts, feelings, and roles you play) come and go, the camera—the ever-present awareness—is always rolling.

This camera captures the entire spectacle without judgment or interference. It remains an unchanging witness to the unfolding drama.

Embracing Impermanence:

Just as in a movie where scenes transition smoothly from one to another, life too is a continuous flow of experiences. The beauty of this perspective is that it reminds you of the transient nature of every event. Whether it is joy or sorrow, success or failure, each scene is temporary and part of a larger, magnificent narrative. This understanding can free you from the weight of any single moment, as you recognize that nothing is permanent except the ever-present now.

Choosing the Role You Play:

When you view life as a movie, you realize that you are not confined to the script handed to you by external circumstances or past conditioning. You have the power to step back, reframe your experience, and even improvise your role. This creative freedom is an expression of your infinite nature—allowing you to manifest your highest potential without being bound by the limitations of the past or the anxieties of the future.

Practical Application:

To harness this movie-like perspective, take a moment each day to reflect on your experiences as if you were watching them on a screen. Notice the ebb and flow of your thoughts and emotions, and observe how the scenes change. This practice can help you detach from any single narrative and cultivate a sense of humor, wonder, and creativity about your life.

Conclusion

Embracing the eternal now means living with direct, unmediated experience. It is about recognizing that the past and future are not separate destinations but rather aspects of a continuous, ever-present reality. By cultivating immediate awareness, you unlock the power to witness life in its purest form, free from the distortions of thought and judgment.

And by viewing life as an ever-unfolding movie, you tap into your innate creative power, allowing each moment to be a joyful expression of your infinite nature.

As you integrate these insights into your daily practice, you'll find that your experience of life transforms. The eternal now becomes your playground, a space where every moment is filled with possibility, clarity, and deep, abiding peace.

Chapter 9

Integration:

From Effortless Being to Engaged Living

INTEGRATION IS THE ART of bringing the serene, boundless nature of your infinite self into every moment of your daily life. In this chapter, we explore how to remain rooted in effortless being while actively engaging with the world around you. You will discover practical methods for balancing presence with action, along with strategies that help you create a life that truly reflects your inner essence.

Balancing Presence with Action in Daily Life

Life in the world is dynamic, full of events, responsibilities, and interactions. Yet, your true nature is not confined to the roles you play or the busyness of daily activities—it is an ever-present, expansive awareness. The challenge lies in harmonizing the calm of effortless being with the energy of engagement.

❖ Mindful Action:

Every action, from a simple conversation to tackling a complex project at work, can become an opportunity to express your true nature. Instead of acting from a state of stress or distraction, bring a mindful attention to each task. When you choose to act with full awareness, you transform routine activities into expressions of your infinite being.

❖ The Practice of Pause:

Cultivate small pauses throughout your day—moments where you simply breathe and return to the present. These brief interludes remind you that while the external world may be in constant motion, your inner state remains steady and vast.

Whether you're transitioning between meetings, commuting, or even waiting in line, use these pauses to reconnect with the sense of calm that is always within you.

- ❖ **Flow and Flexibility:**

Recognize that action need not be at odds with presence. In fact, when you are fully present, you move through life with a natural ease.

Allow yourself the flexibility to adapt to challenges without losing sight of your inner stillness. This means being open to unexpected changes while maintaining a grounded, centered state—where every decision is made from a place of clarity rather than reactive impulse.

Practical Strategies for Living Your True Nature

Transforming your life into an authentic expression of effortless being doesn't require grand gestures—often, it's the small, consistent practices that lead to profound shifts.

- ❖ **Daily Mindfulness Practices:**

Start and end your day with a few minutes of meditation or conscious breathing. These moments serve as anchors that remind you of your true, unchanging essence. Even during busy periods, a brief mindfulness check—simply noticing the breath or observing your thoughts without judgment—can help you stay connected to your inner state.

❖ **Using Impersonal Language:**

When stressful thoughts or emotions arise, reframe them in impersonal terms. For example, instead of saying, "I'm angry" or "I feel hurt," notice, "There is impersonal awareness of anger" or "There is awareness of a feeling of hurt." This simple shift helps you detach from reactive identification, allowing you to witness experiences without getting entangled in them.

❖ **Reflective Journaling:**

Write down your experiences, especially moments when you notice a tug between your true nature and the demands of daily life. Journaling can help you track recurring patterns or "invitations" that pull you into dualistic thinking. Over time, this practice strengthens your ability to recognize and gently decline those invitations, reinforcing your commitment to effortless being.

❖ **Regular Energy Check-Ins:**

Create a habit of asking yourself, "Am I feeling expansive or contracted right now?" Notice the sensations in your body and the quality of your thoughts. If you sense contraction (a sign of stress or identification with limiting beliefs), use your preferred mindfulness technique to shift back into a state of expansion. This ongoing practice serves as a constant reminder that you have the power to choose your state of being.

Creating a Life That Reflects Your Infinite Being

When your daily actions and choices are aligned with the truth of who you are, your external life naturally begins to mirror that inner clarity and freedom.

❖ **Living Authentically:**

True integration means that your external lifestyle—your work, relationships, creative pursuits—reflects the effortless state within. Instead of forcing outcomes or striving against the current, allow life to unfold in accordance with your inner guidance.

Notice how your choices, when made from a place of presence rather than from the pressure to perform, create an authentic and fulfilling existence.

❖ **Manifesting with Ease:**

Recognize that the power to create comes from the same source as your effortless being. By shifting from a mindset of striving (which is often fueled by fear and lack) to one of playful creation, you invite opportunities that are naturally in line with your highest self.

This doesn't mean that nothing ever challenges you; rather, it means that you approach challenges with a deep trust in the underlying intelligence and love that sustains all life.

❖ Harmonizing Inner and Outer Worlds:

View every aspect of your life as a canvas upon which your infinite being is expressed. Your career, home, social interactions, and creative endeavors are not separate from you—they are extensions of your inner state. When you cultivate a life that mirrors the ease and joy of your effortless being, you create an environment that supports not only your own growth but also inspires those around you.

❖ Living with Intentional Joy:

The journey of integration invites you to be intentional about your experience. Choose activities, relationships, and environments that uplift you. Surround yourself with people and practices that reinforce the understanding that you are not bound by struggle, but rather, you are here to enjoy the beauty of existence.

Celebrate the small moments of bliss and the seamless interplay between effortlessness and action.

Conclusion

Integration is not about withdrawing from the world—it is about stepping into it fully, with the profound awareness of who (or rather, what) you truly are. As you balance presence with action, use practical strategies to maintain connection with your infinite self, and allow your life to naturally reflect that truth, you begin to live in a state of harmony that transcends the dualistic matrix.

In this state, every moment is an opportunity to manifest joy, creativity, and boundless possibility—transforming the ordinary into an extraordinary expression of your true nature.

Chapter 10

True Peace at Last:

Living the Infinite Being Experience

AS WE REACH THE CONCLUSION of this journey, we stand at a threshold where the old patterns of seeking have been replaced by the effortless state of being. This chapter is an invitation to pause, reflect, and embrace the truth that has always been present beneath the shifting appearances of life.

In these final reflections, we honor the transformation that has taken place and set our sights on a future defined not by struggle, but by an abiding peace and boundless freedom.

Final Reflections on the Journey

Over the course of this book, you have navigated the terrain from the restless pursuit of fulfillment to the serene recognition of your infinite, impersonal nature. Each chapter has been a stepping stone from the stirring realization that "there has to be more to life" to the deep dive into practical techniques for declination of the dualistic invitations that once held you captive.

Now, as we reflect on the journey, consider the following:

A Shift in Perception:

What once felt like a constant battle against limitation has transformed into a gentle awareness that every moment is complete as it is. The constant chatter of the mind has given way to a spacious silence—a silence that affirms your true nature is ever-present and unchanging.

The Unfolding of Awareness:

The experiences recounted in these pages are not fleeting moments of inspiration but enduring pointers to the reality of effortless being. Each realization, each tool that helped you move beyond the confines of the personal, is a testament to the deep truth that you are not defined by transient thoughts or emotions.

Integration and Authenticity:

The journey has been one of integration: merging the insights of direct, embodied experience with the wisdom of intellectual knowing. This synthesis has led you to a place where life itself is experienced as an unfolding masterpiece—a movie where every scene is infused with meaning, even if the plot is ever-changing.

The End of Suffering and the Beginning of True Freedom

Imagine a life where the incessant pull of negative emotions, self-doubt, and relentless striving no longer dictate your every moment. Here, in the state of effortless being, suffering loses its grip because its very foundation—the belief in a separate, limited self—has been dismantled.

No More Chasing After Happiness:

True freedom arises when you realize that happiness is not something to be attained or produced; it is the natural state of your infinite being. The struggles of the past—where you constantly sought to fix, improve, or escape your circumstances—dissipate when you simply rest in the knowing that you already are complete.

Releasing the Chains of Duality:

The dualistic matrix, with all its invitations to fear, anxiety, and self-doubt, has lost its power. When you stand firmly in the awareness of your infinite nature, these triggers become nothing more than passing thoughts. They no longer have the ability to rob you of your peace because you recognize them as merely part of the background noise of existence.

An Invitation to True Freedom:

With the cessation of suffering comes a profound liberation—a freedom to experience life without the burden of constant expectation or regret. This is not a future promise; it is the here and now. Your inner freedom is the foundation upon which a joyful, creative, and dynamic life is built.

A Call to Live from Your True Nature

Now, as you close this book and step back into the flow of your daily life, remember that every moment is an opportunity to live in alignment with your infinite being. The insights, tools, and reflections you have encountered are not merely theoretical they are practical, living guides that can inform each decision, each action, each breath you take.

Embrace the Effortless:

Let go of the need to constantly strive for something external. Recognize that the effortless state of being is your natural habitat.

As you interact with the world—whether in work, relationships, or creative endeavors—allow your inner clarity and ease to shine through, transforming every experience into an expression of your true self.

Live Authentically and Boldly:

Step into your life with a deep trust in the wisdom of your infinite nature. Every challenge and every triumph is a moment to express the truth of what you are. Your journey is not about escaping the world; it is about engaging with it from a place of profound peace and love.

Inspire Others Through Your Example:

As you embody this state of effortless being, you become a living beacon for those still caught in the struggle of duality. Your life, lived from the center of infinite awareness, offers a powerful testament to the possibility of true freedom—a freedom that is available to everyone, if only they dare to remember who (or rather, what) they truly are.

Conclusion

True Peace at last is not an endpoint, but an ever-present reality waiting to be embraced. The infinite being experience is not a destination to be reached but the inherent truth of your existence. As you move forward, let this deep sense of peace guide you, reminding you with every breath that you are not limited by the transient phenomena of the world.

You are the eternal, boundless presence that underlies all change—and in that truth, you will find the freedom to live, love, and create without constraint.

May this realization serve as your constant companion, lighting the path toward a life filled with joy, creativity, and an unwavering peace that transcends all understanding.

True Peace at last, indeed.

Continue Your Journey with Additional Resources & a Personal Invitation

THANK YOU SO MUCH for your interest in exploring the path of Effortless Being. As you continue your journey toward realizing your infinite nature, I wanted to share some additional resources that have helped me along the way—and I hope they'll inspire you, too.

Books & Media

Awakening to Effortless Being: My previous book details my personal journey from striving in the dualistic world to realizing the effortless, infinite nature that underlies all experience. I invite you to dive into its pages to discover practical pointers for living from your true self.

Effortless Being Channel on YouTube: I regularly share interviews, coaching calls, and discussions on living from a place of pure presence. If you haven't already, please check out the channel for insights and inspiring conversations that can help shift your focus from struggle to joyful, effortless creation.

Additional Resources

For further information and deeper understanding, I recommend your exploring the work of David Bingham. Go to www.David Bingham.org and his YouTube Channel, David Bingham, where I learned my true nature.

A Personal Invitation

I also believe that sometimes a one-on-one conversation can make all the difference on this path. If you'd like to discuss your journey further, ask questions, or simply connect on a deeper level, please feel free to contact me directly. I'd be honored to set up a personal call with you to explore how you can live more effortlessly and in alignment with your infinite nature.

You can reach me at: infinitebeingness1@gmail.com

Thank you again for joining me on this journey. I look forward to connecting with you—on the channel, through my writings, or one-on-one.

Warm regards,

Robert Rugg

YouTube handle: @effortlessbeing5162

ROBERT RUGG

Acknowledgments

I WOULD LIKE TO EXPRESS my deepest gratitude to everyone who has supported and inspired me on this journey toward effortless being. This book is a culmination of many years of exploration, insight, and personal transformation, and I am honored to share it with you.

A special thank you goes to David Bingham. His profound insight—that "you are the infinite being having a human experience," as he so beautifully expressed in *The Greatest Secret*—resonated with me on a deep level and was instrumental in my own awakening. His gentle guidance, both through his writings and his engaging YouTube channel, has illuminated the path for countless seekers, myself included.

I am especially grateful for his gracious contribution in writing the forward for my previous book, *Awakening to*

Effortless Being: Realizing Your Infinite Self. His words not only affirmed my vision but also enriched the spiritual tapestry of my work.

I also wish to acknowledge the many friends, teachers, and fellow travelers who have shared their wisdom and encouragement along the way. Your insights, support, and the collective energy of our community have been a constant source of inspiration and strength.

Thank you all for being a part of this journey. It is my sincere hope that this book serves as a beacon of light, empowering each reader to discover and embrace their true, effortless nature.

With infinite gratitude,
 Robert Rugg
 Effortless Being Publications

About the Author

ROBERT RUGG IS ALSO known as Liquid Sunshine, inspired by Abraham Hicks's words, "You feel like liquid sunshine." He is a writer, coach, and joy enthusiast whose work is inspired by the teachings of David Bingham and the profound realization of infinite being.

After experiencing a life-changing shift in perspective from the words, *"You are the infinite being having a human experience,"* Robert felt a calling to share the joy, alignment, and clarity that come from living in the flow.

INFINITE BEING

With a passion for uplifting and inspiring others, Robert Rugg has created books, a YouTube channel, and one-on-one coaching experiences that help people reconnect with their inner being and manifest a life of ease and abundance. His lighthearted, humorous approach to spirituality reminds readers and viewers alike that life is meant to be fun, expansive, and full of surprises—much like the playful style that inspired Liquid Sunshine.

When not writing or coaching, Robert enjoys spending time with his wife and daughters—Brianna, Madison, and Abby—traveling to Abraham Hicks workshops, and living each day with the mantra: *"I'm here, I feel good, and I hope you do, too."*

Connect with Robert Rugg on YouTube at Effortless Being.

Contact:

📧 Email: infinitebeingness1@gmail.com

📺 YouTube: @EffortlessBeing5162

Printed in Great Britain
by Amazon